Laser Focus SEO for Niche Sites

Explained:

How I ranked my 19 sites to top 10

in Google

I0478551

by

George M. Lambert

Published by CSB Academy Publishing Co.

CSB Academy

Disclaimer

The information, statements and opinions expressed in this eBook are only intended as a guide to some of the important considerations to be taken into account relating to SEO for niche sites. We do not accept liability for any loss, damage or other consequences that may arise as a result of any person acting on or using the information and opinions discussed within this book.

Laser Focus SEO for Niche Sites Explained:

How I ranked my 19 sites to top 10 in Google

Table of Contents

A personal thanks for buying my book. I would love to hear your feedback. To show my appreciation, I have decided to offer everyone that buys my book a Free copy of all future updated edition of this book. To receive this please register your name at: WWW.FreelanceSEOservices.net

Introduction. ANYONE Can Do This!!!

Firstly, I'd like to thank you for taking the time to read this book. I know that you probably have a to-do list that is every growing, and that it can be difficult to get a few moments to yourself, let alone dive into the virtual or real pages of an book. However, I want to assure you that by taking the valuable time to read this, you will be justly rewarded. This guide is going to provide you with the ability to bring in extra income and maybe even give you the opportunity to turn niche site building into a profitable business venture, even if you have no prior internet marketing experience.

I know what you might be thinking right about now: "oh, no...not another book about using a 'fail proof' system that is just going to fall short of expectations in the end". I want to reassure you that this is NOT one of those kinds of books. As a matter of fact, I've done absolutely everything that I am going to suggest to you herein, and know that these techniques and ideas can help you to drive traffic to your niche sites and significantly boost your online revenue. If you are willing to put in the time and effort, you have the power to transform your niche sites into a lucrative online empire. I did it, and so can you.

Like many people, I have spent most of my adult life looking for a way that I could earn a decent living, and still have time to enjoy the proverbial "fruits of my labor". I've held jobs that paid me just enough to get by, but just didn't provide me with the chance to have any sort of personal life. After working long hours and having to deal with an enormous amount of pressure, I'd make just enough to survive, rather than actually being able to live the life that I wanted. At the end of the day, I'd come home completely exhausted, and unable to really do anything but sleep and prepare for the next morning, when I would have to carry out the same routine all over again.

I thought that was all going to change when I landed my "dream" job in the corporate world. I knew that I would have to work hard, but that I would be able to build up a nice little nest egg, so that I could actually enjoy the finer things in life. I truly believed that this was going to be my opportunity to work toward my financial goals and really be able to stop worrying about paying the bills and covering my basic expenses. Now that I had a great job that offered my good pay, benefits, and a wide range of other perks, I was finally able to live my life and feel secure about my financial future. All of that changed when I lost my corporate job in 2011...

I was called into the HR manager's office and told that they were "cutting back", and that I was one of the many who was being laid off. I was devastated. It wasn't just that I was losing my job, it was that I was losing that sense of security that I'd always wanted. I was going to have to give up that steady income, and once more join the countless other people who were looking for work in a down economy. And that's when I decided to try my luck at something completely different than I'd been doing: making money online.

I began perusing the web for online money making opportunities. I tried to look for a way to earn a good living, without having to spend sixteen hours a day away from home at a job (or two). I scoured online message boards to try and find the perfect opportunity. I even went so far as to look into various different schemes and systems that you always see advertised online. However, everything that I came across seemed to either involve a sizable investment up-front, or just didn't produce the results that they promised. Just when I thought that online ventures weren't going to be the answer, I came up with the idea of internet marketing and niche site building. Mind you, I had absolutely no experience with either and didn't know the first thing about how to create revenue generating sites, let alone how to carry out effective SEO.

As a result, I first failed miserably at the whole endeavor. Looking back, I am certain that it can be attributed to one major issue: I just didn't know the importance of SEO (search engine optimization). I knew some of the basic principles of SEO, but simply wasn't aware of how crucial an SEO strategy was in the grand scheme of things.

So, I took it upon myself to learn more about search engine optimization, and studied on my own by soaking up information from anything and everything I could get my hands on. After 2 online courses, 7 books, and 3 months of researching on Google non-stop, I I learned what SEO is and how to actually implement it on my sites.

One thing that I noticed while I was trying to conduct as

much research as possible was that there is not one book that talks about the bigger picture for a niche site SEO, nor one that pin-points the steps that you should take to become successful via SEO niche sites. That's why I've decided to write this book. I don't want anyone to have to go through what I went through to gain an in depth understanding of search engine optimization for the niche site market. So, I thought it would be a good idea to share my knowledge and insights that I've gathered along the way with you.

I am here to tell you that ANYONE can use an effective SEO strategy to build informative and money making niche sites. I didn't have any background whatsoever in marketing, online income generation, or SEO development when I began my niche site venture. In fact, I was probably the last person who you'd think would ever be able to pull something like this off (thanks to my lack of experience in the industry). So far, I've been able to use SEO to make my 23 sites a success. Out of those 23 sites, 19 of them are now ranking between the 1st and the 8th on Google, and the last 4 are only between a month and 3 months old at the time of this writing.

Even if you've never tried to create niche sites before, or if you have been hesitant to try to find effective ways to generate online revenue (due to all of the horror stories that you hear about getting scammed online or having to invest large sums of money for very little return), I can assure you that using SEO for niche sites will provide you with a significant opportunity. It did for me, and it can most definitely do the same for you.

This is where you now have a unique advantage. In this book I am going to show you how you can become a successful niche site marketer. As a matter of fact, I am taking it a step further and will be sharing valuable advice, such as keyword research tips and how to build a site from an SEO stand point, that I have found helpful throughout my internet marketing career. These tips are time tested and proven (and the result of much trial and error on my part). I am giving you the rare chance to learn from my mistakes, and to benefit financially from the experience that I've gained.

So, if you've been looking for an all in one resource for SEO niche site creation and marketing, then you've found it. I am going to share insider secrets with you, in order to give you the ability to potentially turn your site into a steady stream of income. By utilizing the ideas the techniques that can be found herein, you can become the next in the long line of entrepreneurs who has transformed their interest, hobby, creative idea, or passion into an online money making opportunity.

Consider this to be your all inclusive guide through the virtual world of SEO niche marketing, complete with a variety of informative and helpful advice and tips. The first thing that I'll go over is exactly what is Niche Site SEO and how it is different from other forms of search engine optimization.

Chapter 1. What is SEO for Niche Sites?

Before we dive into the basics of SEO marketing for niche sites, I thought it was important to first explain exactly what niche site SEO is, and how it differs from other sites. Search engine optimization is a vast topic and even more time consuming work than writing the actual content for your site. SEO, simply put, is the hardest part of site building process. However, my main focus in this book is to explain how SEO can be vastly different for a Niche site as compared to an authority site.

You see, not all SEO is created equal. Techniques that might work for an authority site just aren't going to be as effective for niche sites. Here is a brief explanation of the key differences between the two most common types of websites, in terms of SEO strategies:

Authority Websites...

- Target a wide range of keywords (potentially thousands), that cover various different subjects within a particular niche.

- Become highly trusted sites that, as the name suggests, tends to be an "authority" on the topic. Therefore, they can achieve high rankings in Google.

- Takes a great amount of time to perfect strategy and generate traffic, given that there are so many keywords involved.

Niche Websites...

- Target one keyword (a few at the most), that pertains to one particular niche topic.

- Aims to rank high in the search engines for a carefully selected long tail keyword.

- Can begin driving traffic to the site almost immediately if the right keyword is chosen.

Whenever I think of SEO niche sites versus authority sites a popular saying comes to mind: "A jack of all trades, but master at none". An authority site generally takes a long time to become successful and lucrative. You have to work on creating content that includes all of the various keywords that you've chosen, but can never really focus on bringing in visitors based upon just a handful of keywords. On the other hand, a niche site allows you to really explore multiple different subjects that fall under the purview of your selected keyword(s), so that you can concentrate on attracting visitors who are searching for that particular and very specific topic or subject within a niche.

Rather than having to constantly post new content that features new keywords, you can create a handful of great articles or content pages for the site that can go a long way in terms of niche SEO. This means that you won't have to constantly provide fresh content for the site, and can work on slowly but surely building a niche site empire, wherein you can eventually have a myriad of niche sites that are bringing in traffic and increasing your Adsense or affiliate marketing revenue on a continual basis.

White Hat SEO vs. Black Hat SEO

Another important SEO topic that I wanted to cover before we delve into niche SEO tactics is White Hat vs. Black Hat SEO. You'll probably hear these terms quite often while you are doing your research, so I thought it was wise if I talked a bit about them here. In a nutshell, Black hat SEO should be avoided altogether. It can only lead to trouble for your niche site, given that Google tends to penalize sites that use black hat SEO tactics.

Essentially, White Hat SEO involves seamless keyword integration. The words fit naturally into the text, and the content itself is informative and helpful for the reader. There isn't any over usage of the keyword(s), and the meta-tags are relevant. These sites are the ones that make it to the top of the rankings, especially now that Google has updated its system (which I'll talk about later in this chapter).

At the other end of the spectrum you'll find Black Hat SEO, which includes keyword stuffing (using the keyword more often than you should), cloaked pages, hidden text links, and tags that have absolutely nothing to do with the content provided. These kind of SEO tactics can also involve automated programs, wherein those practicing Black Hat SEO can build 3000 backlinks that are submitted in just two hours. These kinds of underhanded techniques typically lead to a site getting banned by Google, or they can be penalized by lowered rankings in the search engines.

The Impact of Google Updates Upon Niche Site SEO

This brings me to my final point in this chapter: how Google updates can affect your SEO strategy. Previous Google updates have included "Panda" and "Penguin", and have changed the way that SEO works in many ways. The most significant change has come in the form of penalization for sites that don't provide high quality content or stuff their content with keywords. These sites are often either completely removed from result listings or lowered in ranking.

Sites that aren't affected by these changes are ones that already provide exceptional content that has been well researched, and incorporate keywords into that content in a natural way.

Google Hummingbird update and Niche Site SEO

Around its 15th Birthday Google released it's new search algorithm which like before they named it after a cute little animal, this time it is call Hummingbird. But unlike before this is not just an update on the existing search algorithm, instead it is a whole new search algorithm all together. According to some known SEO experts like David Amerland *"Hummingbird is a definite expansion of Google's semantic capability evident at the search interface level that reveals, significantly, two things, First, Google has increased its ability to deal with complex search queries which means that it also has got better at indexing entities in Web documents. Second, it has got a lot better at relationally linking search queries and Web documents which means that its Knowledge Graph must be considerably enriched."*

He also goes on to explain how Google's move towards semantic search with benefit our everyday SEO practices

"From a strategy point of view this opens the horizon for companies and webmasters considerably. From a practical perspective, the need to identify the USP of each business and become authoritative within it is now a key criteria for continued SEO success. The comparison element that has been integrated suggests that semantic mark-up may begin to confer an advantage now when it comes to helping index information in products and services."

So Google is moving towards Semantic search, what is semantic search you ask? Here is the classic text book definition from Wikipedia.

"Semantic search seeks to improve search accuracy by understanding searcher intent and the contextual meaning of terms as they appear in the searchable dataspace, whether on the Web or within a closed system, to generate more relevant results. Author Seth Grimes lists "11 approaches that join semantics to search", and Hildebrand et al. provide an overview that lists semantic search

systems and identifies other uses of semantics in the search process. Semantic search systems consider various points including context of search, location, intent, variation of words, synonyms, generalized and specialized queries, concept matching and natural language queries to provide relevant search results. Major web search engines like Google and Bing incorporate some elements of semantic search."

In layman's term Google search engine is becoming more like a human and how we think. Instead of focusing on a specific word out a whole search query it is instead trying to find the meaning of the whole sentence as a whole. Semantic and Natural are the new focus for Google when it comes to SEO. meaning everything you do to improve SEO has to look natural and semantic but never artificial. Let me explain more, let's say you are crazy about rose gardening and you decided to share your knowledge with the whole world. So you decided to start a blog, but you didn't know anything about SEO nor you wanted to make money from the site. All you do is report every week what and how you did what you did for your rose garden that past week. You added many pictures to show your success, you also have some people that comment on your work or ask you for advice some of which found you from your Facebook or twitter since you linked them together. In a year time you became an authority in rose gardening without you even knowing. Suddenly you install Google analytics and found out you have 3000UV everyday to your blog. Well folks that is what Natural and semantic is all about. Google wants us to go back to the basics the way we were and way we should be.

But In niche site business we do not have a year of adding content every week, but what we still have is essentially the same, a SEO optimized site both on and off page, quality content that provides the highest value in your niche, some quality back links pointing to and from your site and the power of social media. We can still speed up that one year process into 30-60 days.

Since this new update content is once again became the KING. Your content has to be relevant, has to provide the highest quality value to readers and match closely with the query. As I said before we are going back to the basics. Rather than using ranking algorithms such as Google's Page Rank to predict relevancy, semantic search uses semantics, or the science of meaning in language, to produce highly relevant search results. In most cases, the goal is to deliver the information queried by a user rather than have a user sort through a list of loosely related keyword results.

So, what does this mean for your niche site business and the future of Internet marketing? Not a lot if you have been paying attention. The previous Panda and Penguin updates taught us one thing about Internet marketing — the sites producing the best quality content for the needs of their audience will have the easiest time garnering organic traffic. The Hummingbird update is the logical next step towards separating the best material from junk of the

Internet.

As I said before this update will put less emphasis on matching keywords and more emphasis on understanding what a user is most likely trying to obtain in his or her search results. If I can give niche site developers one piece of advice after this update, it's to prioritize a well-rounded online marketing strategy that continues to deliver a clear message with a lot of value for their readers.. Every business has an audience, but not every business understands the needs of their audience. If you as a internet marketer can prioritize the needs of your reader/users and create content to satisfy those needs than you will see the biggest success in very near future.

The days of 1 or 2 page site with EMD (Exact match domain) and couple of over optimized long tail keywords are over. No more shortcuts, if you want to be successful in this business you have to go in for the long haul. Build quality sites that provides the ultimate value to the end users.

Therefore, in order to avoid your site being banned from the major search engines, such as Google, you'll have to always insure that you have high quality content on your site, and that you limit the usage of keywords. As such, if you want to always stay on the good side of Google and the other major search engine platforms, you'll have to follow the aforementioned "rules". I'll discuss this later on in the book in depth.

Chapter 2. Keyword Research and its Importance

Now is the moment that you've all been waiting for...let's dive into the first step in niche site SEO: keyword research. Before you even begin to build your site or select the domain name, let's understand that this is THE most important part of your niche site business. Once you settle upon a certain keyword or keywords, there is no turning back. Therefore, it's crucial that you are aware of just how important keyword research is and how vital the right keywords are to the success of your niche site.

I cannot stress this enough...keyword research is THE most important part of your SEO strategy. Above all else, you need to be sure that you invest a good deal of time into finding which keyword(s) is right for your niche site, and which will generate the most traffic (which equates to increased online ad revenue). Here are just a few of the ways that you conduct keyword research on your own:

- Enlisting the aid of SEO keyword software like Long tail Pro or Market Samurai are great options, as they can allow you to see which keywords are the most competitive. In essence, these sites give you the opportunity to search SEO stats for other popular sites in your niche. For example, if you have a site that is going to be dedicated to container herb gardening and are thinking about using that as a keyword, you can type in the long tail keyword and view other sites that have targeted that particular phrase. You can then see their page authority rank, number of page links, and even the site's age. This will enable you to see what the competition is doing, and to fine tune a strategy that will work best for you.

- Use Google trends, Google keyword suggestion tool, and Google instant to come up with some niche ideas. Google trends is particularly helpful, as it will allow you to find out what topics are hot right now, so that you can build a niche site around a popular niche or subject. For instance, if you notice that there has been an ongoing trend around a particular type of video game, you can potentially begin a niche site that focuses on a keyword that will draw in visitors who are looking for information about that specific topic.

I mentioned page rank and age site just a moment ago, and would like to touch on those subjects briefly. Below you'll find an image from Long Tail Pro (which I referenced earlier). You'll notice that there are a wide range of criteria listed at the top of the web page:

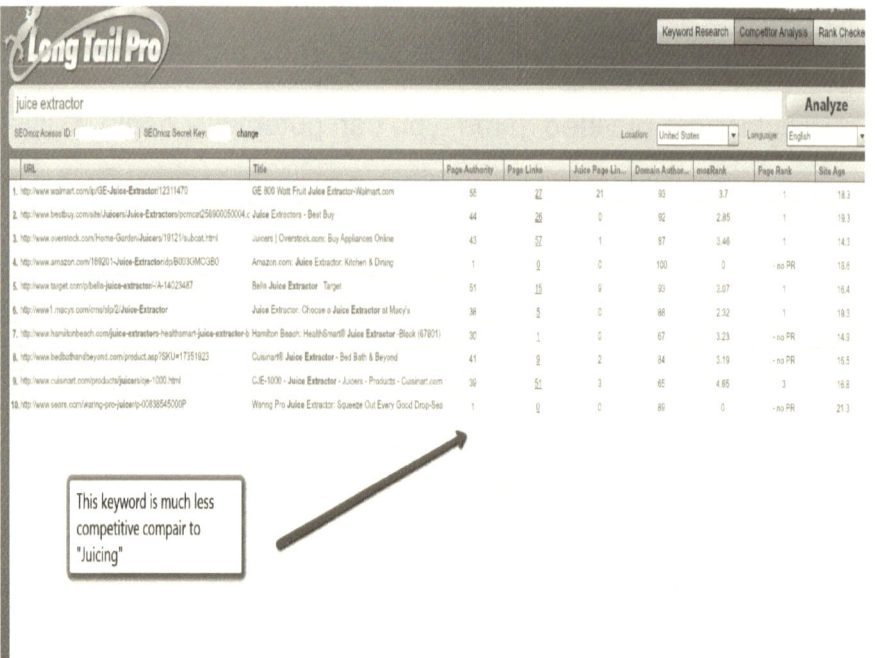

All of these have a direct impact upon your SEO strategy and keyword research. For example, the age of the site of your competitor can give you an idea of how established the site is. The "page authority" can allow you to gauge how successful the site in terms of keyword usage. Overall, you will be able to tell exactly how competitive a keyword is, as compared to another keyword. For example, the keyword "juice extractor" is far less competitive than "juicing", judging by the chart above and the one below. The web page image below is based upon the "juicing" primary keyword.

You'll notice in this image that the top 10 results are much more competitive, given that the top "page authority" ranking here is 32 ,as opposed to the previous image (wherein the top ranking for "juice extractor" was the coveted number 1 spot).

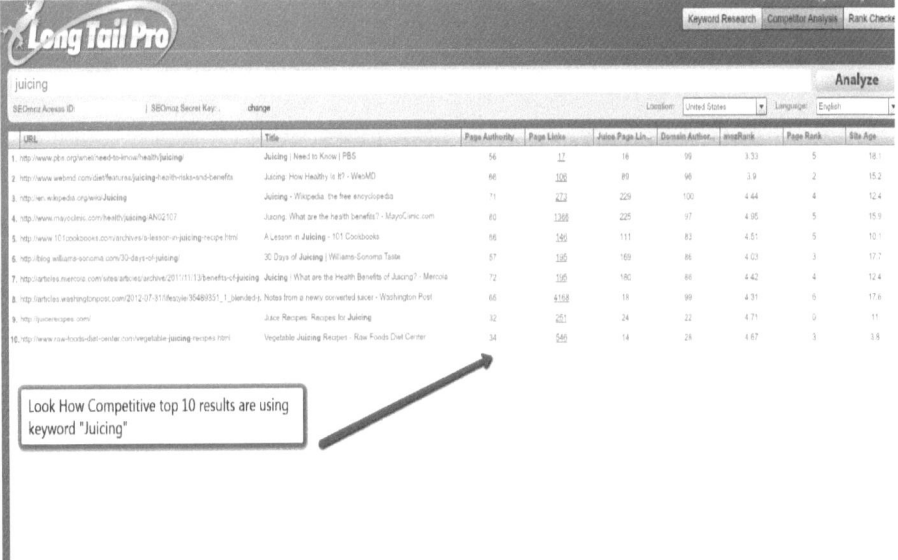

Look How Competitive top 10 results are using keyword "Juicing"

One of the most helpful searches that you can carry out on sites like Long Tail Pro is exact keyword competition, based upon a keyword of your choice. For example, in the image below I've input "Juicing for weight loss" as my keyword. The keyword "juicing" is highly competitive, based upon the fact that it has roughly 27100 local searches and 1.23 is the average cost per click (CPC), which comes into play when you're talking about search engine ad spots. On the other hand, the word "vegetable juices" has only 2400 local searches, and a .97 average CPC. Therefore, if you targeted this keyword, you'd have a greater chance of actually beating out the competition and getting valuable traffic to your niche site.

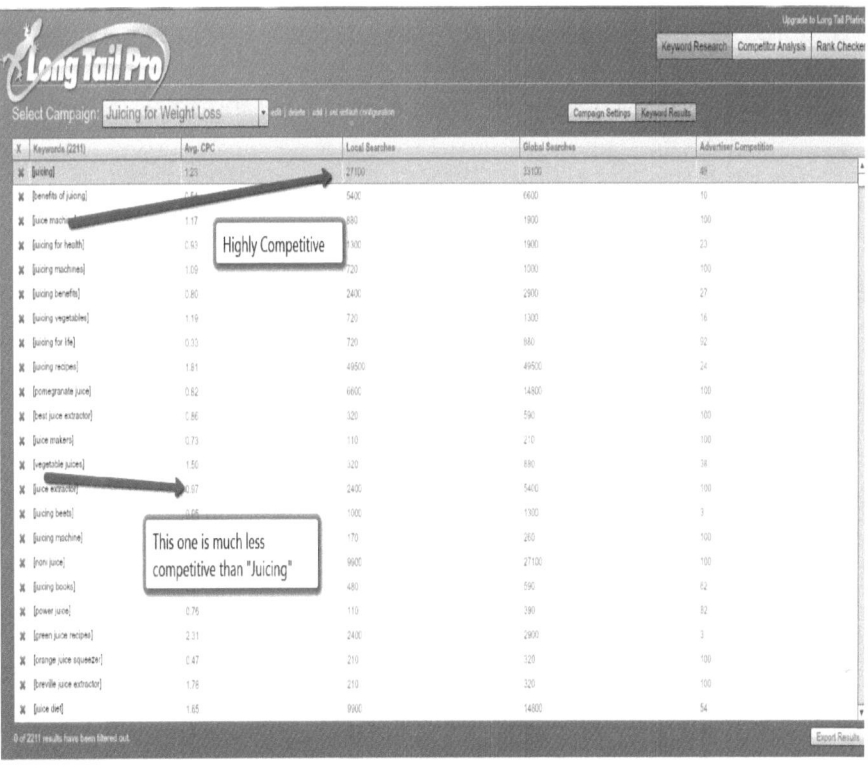

To illustrate this point, I'd like to give you a perfect example of a site where keyword research made a world of difference. It just so happened that this was one of my first sites, and I made a big mistake when it came to picking the niche...

The site was www.bestjuicingpractice.com. I put quite a bit of time and effort into building that site, as I was new to this business and became very inspired by listening to podcasts from Pat Flynn, Chris Guthrie, and Spencer Haws, among many others. One night I was flipping through Netflix and found a documentary called "Fat, Sick and Nearly Dead", and after watching it I felt very inspired about changing my life. I wanted to lead a healthier lifestyle, so I started juicing every day. It became an overnight passion for me. So, it seemed only natural that I would choose the topic as my first niche site business. I figured that I would be able to build a site around juicing and it's real health benefits.

I outsourced the process in sections as I was taught from various podcasts created by experienced niche marketing professionals. I found a great writer who was a Cancer survivor and an avid juicer, She was passionate about the subject, and a true believer in what I was trying to achieve.

As such, we teamed up and she wrote some wonderful content for me, and even ended up penning a book on my behalf.

While doing all this, however, I made one common mistake...I forgot how important keyword research was. This was despite the fact that all of the SEO experts made a point to say in their podcasts that this is absolutely the MOST important part. I remember going into Google ad word keyword tools and typing in 'juicing'. Then, without fully understanding that it's not the domain name that really counts (even though at the time exact match domain did carry some weight), I chose the name "bestjuicingpractice" for my domain. How did I arrive at this selection? Well, I noticed that there were thousands of people searching the term "Juicing" so I said: that's it! I finally found my perfect niche, and now I have the "perfect" domain name. Boy, was I ever wrong...The site received an average of 3-5 visitors a day!

Now, let's now talk about the *2 biggest mistakes* I made (so that you can learn from them and never repeat them with your own niche site)...

1. I picked a niche that is highly competitive. The only way I could have possibly been successful is if I'd have started an authority site and worked at it every day for a year or two...then I may have seen my site rank in the top 10 of Google.

2. I did not understand SEO at all. Even though I hired people to help me build my site and to write content for me, SEO was just something that I didn't budget for. There was no on or off page SEO. Nor did I know how to do link building. Worse still, I started going to Fiverr and seeing $5 deals for some silly SEO tricks and I kept paying them to do work their supposed "magic". All along, I kept telling myself: "hey, I built a beautiful site. I have awesome

content. Google is bound to see me and put me on top of the search results soon". Needless to say, that never did happen.

In the end, I was left with one all-important question: *What could I have done differently?*...

1. Knowing what I know now, I would never get into a competitive niche like weight loss or Juicing for weight loss and such topics. But if I had to, I would spend a day or two and find a micro niche on that vast topic of " juicing for weight loss " and target one long tail keyword which was not as highly competitive. I would have carried out the vital keyword research for "juicing" that I pictured earlier in this chapter. Right away, I would have realized that "juicing" was saturated online, and that "vegetable juices" or "juicing extractor" would have been much better SEO keywords.

2. In terms of SEO tactics, I would have focused on both On and Off page SEO. On page SEO deals with on-site techniques that generate traffic, such as meta-tag usage, having keywords in the title, and optimizing each post. Off page SEO deals more with link building, social bookmarking and, basically, creating a network of links that directs back to your niche site. On page and off page SEO is so important that I've devoted a full section in the book to each, which I'll cover in depth later on.

How to get started with keyword research...

Before you even begin to build your site, you need to make a list of keywords you will be targeting to rank and optimize your site. This is due to the fact that you will need that list of keywords when you install the All in one SEO plug in via WordPress, and will also need it to create content that is keyword-rich. Use the aforementioned tools and sites to build a comprehensive list of possible keywords, and then narrow down that list to just a few of the most effective keywords. This will allow you to truly focus on the words and phrases that are more likely to drive traffic to your niche site.

Oh, and just to show you how effective the strategies I'm outlining in this book truly are: I wanted to mention a small note about my "failed" site. I decided to take the failure of my juicing site as a challenge, and it now it ranks around 4th or 5th on the top of Google. So, I am on the top 10, which is, of course, where you always want to be. This is a perfect example of how an effective SEO strategy and careful keyword selection can make or break a site's rankings.

Chapter 3. Site building from an SEO point of view

Now that you've picked out your golden nugget, "the keyword", it's time to move onto the next aspect of SEO niche site SEO, which is building the site with search engine optimization in mind. You see, the mistake that most web creators new to the world of niche sites make is to design a site based upon aesthetics alone. They tend to adhere to the belief that a site that looks good is going to bring in scores of visitors. However, a beautifully designed site will not be effective, whatsoever, if you don't integrate SEO from the very beginning.

You'll need to get your domain and arrange for hosting, then install word press. While there may be a myriad of other free website design platforms online, WordPress is the one you'll want to go with. This is primarily due to the fact that it makes SEO implementation a whole lot easier, thanks to its wide range of plug-ins and themes. Make sure to pick out a theme that fits your need properly though.

Even if a theme may be eye-catching and in-line with your niche, it also has to have the right theme and functionality. If you know your monetization strategy, then it is easier to pick the right theme. For example if you are monetizing with Amazon than pick a theme that is made for Amazon affiliates is ideal. If your method is ad sense, then pick something that allows easy ad placement.

Below is an example of a WordPress theme that has Adsense already built-in. This will allow for you to easily link your Adsense account, then begin generating revenue via your niche site almost immediately.

You'll notice in the image above that there is room for 3 ads on the page, which is typically the maximum you are allotted. There is one area at the top, and then additional Adsense sections on either side of the content.

Next, you need to make sure you understand the importance of having the right plug ins installed on your site. WordPress offers countless plugins that can help you to make the most of your niche site and bring in maximized revenue. There are a few plug ins, however, that I think are absolutely "a must have" for every site:

- All in One SEO Pack or Yoast SEO plug in(More hummingbird friendly), which helps ON-page SEO
- Google xml Site Maps
- A Plug in for Google Analytics (so that you can keep track of visitor and site stats)
- A Spam blocker (Akismet is a great anti-spam plugin)
- A site back-up plug in ("Back up Word Press" and "Secure Word Press" are two good   options for this)
- A Plug in for Privacy Policy (such as "Easy Privacy Policy")
- "Add this" Social Bookmarking widget (helps you add social bookmarking to a post)

Depending upon your site and the topic you've chosen, you may also want to try the following WordPress Plug-Ins, as well:

- "Pretty Link" or something similar, which allows you to make your longer links more manageable and simplified

- "Uppsite" or another plugin that enables your site to be viewable on a Mobile device, such as a tablet or smart-phone

- "Smart YouTube Pro" or a similar plugin that enables you to insert you Tube video into your blog with ease

- "Flex Slider", which adds a slider onto your niche site

- "Click Bomb Defense", which helps you to avoid receiving too many clicks from one Ip address on your niche site

One of the most convincing arguments for using WordPress plugins on your site is that they allow you to fully optimize your site quickly and efficiently. There are even SEO plugins that enable you to add meta tags and meta descriptions to all of your blog posts, as well as ones that help you to create automatic SEO links. For example, if you are going to include a number of keywords within your post and want each to redirect to a separate URL, the plugin will allow you to assign a website link to each keyword. Then, when you type in the blog post, it will automatically generate a URL link (which is ideal for link building).

As for choosing a theme, that can make a world of difference when it comes to SEO for your niche site. There are certain free WP themes that come with encrypted links that redirect the visitor to a completely unrelated site, while others improperly coded. This can eventually lead to lowered page ranking, thanks to the fact that search engines will be unable to index your site. One of the biggest mistakes that I've seen over the years are themes that don't make good use of heading tags, which can also hurt your SEO efforts. Ideally, you'll want to choose a theme that allows for easy navigation and indexing, and all posts should feature a heading tag (I'll be discussing headings at length in the next chapter).

Remember, it's essential that you really take the time to become acquainted with the WordPress design platform, and that you explore all of the themes an plugins that they offer. This way you can be sure that you are picking the right theme, and incorporating all of the plugins that are going to make SEO much more effective. While the content on your site itself may be of great importance, without a well designed site that includes carefully selected WP themes and plugins, visitors are going to have a hard time finding your site to begin with and your rankings are going to suffer in the long run.

Chapter 4. Site Content from an SEO Point of View

In this section, I'm going to dive into one of the most important aspects of SEO: content. I am sure you have heard many times that Content is the King and, well...it is. Specially since the new Google Hummingbird update content now has become the most important part of your niche site development. Content is why people come to your site, content is why they will stay on your site, and it is also why they will, hopefully, buy from your affiliate links or click on your ads. As such, if the content is cheap and poorly written, then it just simply won't matter how good your design or theme is, or even how well you've optimized your site overall. Bottom line: if your content is lacking, then your site is going to tank. There's no doubt about it.

The key is that your content not only has to be good, but the best, and it has to provide value to your readers. There are plenty of niche sites out there that contain what is often referred to as "fluff". This is content that has no real value. It's stuffed with keywords, in a vain attempt to boost SEO, the content itself doesn't really provide the reader with the information they were looking for, and eventually the search engines penalize these sites because of their usage of Black Hat SEO tactics.

There is a lot of work that goes on behind the scenes to create good content that actually helps SEO, rather than hinders it. All good content must be keyword-rich, but should be over saturated with keywords. Generally, you should include the keyword about 2 ½ times for every 100 words. For example, if you write a blog post on your niche site that is 400 words long, then you would use the keyword 10 times. This is known as the proverbial "sweet spot", as it's a perfect balance of keywords or phrases.

A word that you'll probably hear thrown around quite often is "keyword density". The keyword density is the percentage of times that you include the keyword or phrase in relation to the overall word count. In this case, the keyword density would be 2.5%. Keeping this "magic" number is important because it will help you to avoid over-stuffing your content with keywords (which can lead to lower search engine rankings). Ultimately, search engines like Google want to see content that is natural, not merely for SEO purposes. They don't want to have over saturated sites at the top of the search results page because these are generally seen as lower quality content sites. All the while keep in mind that your content has to have the natural flow, so the readers can enjoy reading the content while finding valuable information that they are looking for.

In order to carry out effective SEO within your content, you'll also need to fully understand a few other key terms. In the beginning, I was completely unaware of just how important the following SEO techniques were. I wondered why, despite my efforts, I just wasn't getting the traffic I needed. Nobody told me that having "anchor text" on my site could significantly boost my search engine rankings, or that "heading tags" were an all-important part of good content SEO. I'm sharing them with you now because these simple (but oh, so essential) things can make a world of difference in regards to your ranking in ALL of the major search engines:

Anchor text- This is a clickable link within your post or web page content that redirects the reader to another page of your site or another website altogether. Anchor text is so important because it not only allows for easier navigation (and can make it easier for your visitors to buy from your affiliates or find another relevant article/post about the topic), but it also allows you to rank higher. In essence, search engines use anchor links to gauge the subject of a web page when they are ranking sites. So, if you have keywords that double as anchor text, then you have a higher chance of ranking for that particular keyword in the search results.

Heading tags- These are tags in the coding of your site that are used to set the titles (or headers) of your post or web page apart from the body of your content. The most important heading tag is known as "H1", which descends in order of importance until you get to "H6". However, on your niche site you will generally only go up to "H3". The search engines will send out their "bots" to check the relevancy of a particular heading tag in regards to the content itself. Therefore, it's vital that you use related header tags, as this will have a direct impact upon your ranking.

The H1 tag should always contain a basic description of the content that you have featured on the page. It should also include the keyword, and be relevant to the post or article. The H2 heading is generally known as a "sub heading". It is not typically as important as the first header tag, but should still contain the keyword (as it is taken into consideration when the search engines are ranking). I think it's important to also mention that there should only be one H1 tag per page, but there can multiple H2 tags.

Here is an example of heading tags for a juicing niche site (just to give you an idea of how you can use heading tags .For this example, we'll utilize "organic vegetable juicing" as our long tail keyword:

<H1>Organic Vegetable Juicing</H1>
(this would be the title of your post)

<H2>Top 5 Appliances for Organic Vegetable Juicing</H2>
(this would be the first sub-section of your post)

<H2>Tips for Organic Vegetable Juicing</H2>
(this would be the second sub-section of your post)

The Importance of Unique, High Quality Content... It's essential that you take the time and make the effort to create your own quality content. You'd be surprised by how many people just copy and paste from other sites, thinking that they can reap the rewards of another content creators handiwork. The simple truth is that you will get penalized, and any duplicate or private label right content can eventually land your site on the dreaded search engine black list. By using duplicate content, you run the high risk of being banned from search engines or significantly lowering your rank.

If you just don't feel as though you can create quality content, or don't have the time to do so, then why not hire a freelancer to do it for you. There are plenty of sites that offer you the chance to hire professional writers to craft SEO content for your niche site, such as Freelancer, Odesk, Guru, and Elance. If you do hire a writer for your content needs, it is a good idea to check their work for plagiarism by running the article through a plagiarism checker online. Here is a site you can check your VA's work before you pay him.

http://smallseotools.com/plagiarism-checker/

I hired my very first VA (Virtual Assistant) from Elance who designed my first 3 sites. I remember paying him $5 an hour and he took 15-16 hours to build each of the sites. It was not a bad deal than specially since I didn't know how to build a site. One advice on this topic before we move on, try to learn the basics of WordPress site development, no I am not asking you to go buy more books but spend an hour each day for 3-4 days on YouTube. There are plenty of awesome videos that teaches the basics of WordPress site building. This way you can do the minor adjustments like fixing the menu, add articles, add images, tag images, change or add Adsense codes, add Google analytics all of these are very easy and simple task and you do not need a VA to do them for you. What you need help on is SEO, once you have a few sites online, you may see the need to hire a VA who can help you with your SEO needs. I will discuss how you can hire a VA for your SEO needs later in the book. But first you should learn all the SEO tricks and "How to"s yourself, so you can guide your VA properly and not get taken by them.

Integrating Visual SEO... Visual SEO is including images or videos on your site. These can be in the form of photos, graphics, or even YouTube videos that are integrated by using the WordPress plugin I mentioned earlier in the book. When doing this, however, you should always place the keyword in the meta tag of the image. You can add meta data to your images within the image editing software itself, or via WordPress plugin. To do this through your photo editing program, you simply change the description and title of your image, and then insure that this information is also present once you've uploaded it to your WP site.

Remember, no image should be placed on your site without a meta tag. These properly labeled images will help to boost your SEO. Not to mention that it's also visually appealing to the reader and can increase traffic, especially in terms of drawing in readers who may be more visual learners, or even those who simply prefer visual aids. I've included a screen shot of one of my websites below. You'll notice that I've included an image for the post, and have done the same for every other article that has been uploaded to the site. Make sure to pick an image that you can actually use and not break any copyright laws. There are places you can go to find royalty free images for your use. It is not a good idea to just pick out an image from Google image library as most of them are copyrighted images. Also keep in mind that the image you pick out for your article is actually adding some value for the readers, it is giving them a visual idea of what you are talking about in that article.

Here is a site you can go find free images on the net. http://www.sxc.hu

Not only is there an image for every post, but the image contains meta tags, and links to the actual post itself. As such, visitors can easily navigate the site to receive the information that they are looking for, and the meta tags can help me to rank higher.

Submitting to Article Directories... You should also be submitting to at least 3 to 5 articles submission sites. On these sites you can open a free account and submit articles for free, each of which link or refer back to your niche site. This can give you the opportunity to reach an entirely new audience and drive visitors to your site

(visitors who may, very well, click on your affiliate links or

ads).

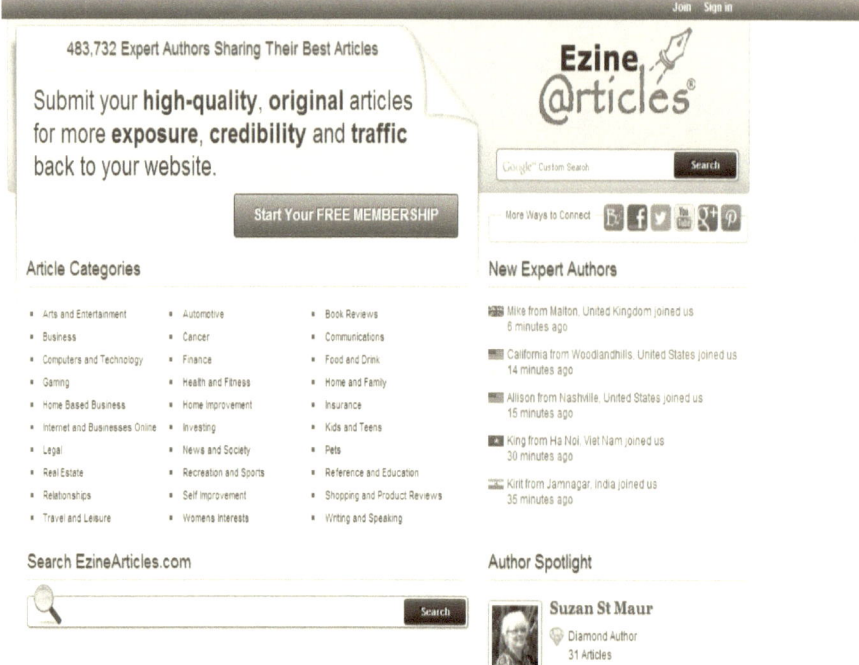

Many people avoid submitting to these sites because they

feel as though they are "giving away" free content.

However, what they are overlooking the fact that these

sites can create new traffic streams, and can serve as an

extension of your SEO network.

When you are submitting to these sites, it's important that you don't upload the same article that you've already posted on your site or offered to other article directory sites. This is considered as duplicate content on the web, which can end up lowering your rankings rather than helping to boost them. Here are some links to some article submission sites that you may find useful:

- E-Zine Articles (http://ezinearticles.com/)

- eHow (http://www.ehow.com/)

- Hub Pages (http://hubpages.com/)

- Squidoo (http://www.squidoo.com/)

- Article Base (http://www.articlesbase.com/)

There's one last thing that I wanted to mention in regards to content SEO, because I feel it's extremely important...You can have too much of a good thing. Now, this may seem like an odd statement, but it's completely relevant. Let me explain: Over optimization is real danger to the success of your niche site. In fact, it can actually harm instead of help your niche site, regardless of your topic.

While overuse of keywords and irrelevant meta tags may help you to boost your traffic temporarily, it will only serve to probably lower your rankings in the long term. If you have too many links on your site, too many H1 tags (or tags that don't really match the content you've provided on your site), or too many keywords throughout your content, you run the risk of over optimizing your site. This is a big "no-no", for lack of a better phrase. So, it's better to just stick to the rules, pay attention to your keyword density, and keep your meta tags in check if you want to stay above board and carry out a highly successful content SEO strategy.

Chapter 5. On-Page SEO

I talked about content SEO in the previous section, which is a big part of On-site search engine optimization, but since the topic is so broad I thought that it was best to dive into On-page SEO here. This form of SEO covers all of the following: the content you post on the site, the title tags, the site's URL, and the image text that you include. In order to have a truly effective on-page SEO strategy, you have to keep all of these things in mind. In essence, you have to focus on the text you provide for your readers and what exactly you are doing to that text that is visible to your readers.

In the old days, only one aspect of on-page SEO really carried any weight in terms of rankings: the behind the scenes techniques. Creating relevant meta tags, concentrating on headers, and anchor text was what got you to the top of the search results. However, thanks to the introduction of Google Panda and Penguin (which I talked about earlier in the book), the quality of the content now plays a HUGE role in rankings. Also, what you include in that content is of the utmost importance now.

In this section, I thought it would be a good idea to just go over some of the basic on-page SEO elements that you should have on your niche site, regardless of what that niche site is about. So, without further ado...here are the 5 most valuable on-page SEO assets that you can have on your website:

Meta Tags. These are special HTML tags that help Google to find your site amongst the millions of other websites out there, and allows for their bots to index your site accordingly. These tags do not appear as text on your site, but are "behind the scenes" descriptors that should always feature your top keywords. They also detail other important information about a web page, such as when it was created, what it's about, and how often you've been updating the site. You can add these meta tags directly into the HTML coding of the site, or (better yet) use a helpful WordPress plugin that can do it for you.

Meta Description. A meta description is, essentially, a meta tag that provides a brief description of your site. It should always feature the keyword, and be to the point. There's no need to mention everything and anything that you've included on your site. In fact, this is generally the text that appears in search engine results. For example, the image below is the search result listing for my juicing site. The description that appears after the date is the meta description. You'll notice that it includes my keyword, which is "best juicing practices".

Best Juicing Practice | How to Loss weight by Juicing - Best Juicers ...
www.**bestjuicingpractice**.com/ ▾
Jun 14, 2013 - BestJuicingPractice.com offers **Best Juicing Practices**. Lose weight, be
healthy and heal from diseases. how to use the best Juicing Extractors ...

The inclusion of the keyword in the meta description is all-important because it helps Google to find you and index you. It also makes your site more relevant for that particular keyword, which means that you'll rank higher.

Keywords in Title and URL. Always (and I mean ALWAYS) put the keyword in both the title and the URL of your site. For the URL, you'll want to use your primary targeted keyword, such as the one you've built your entire niche site around. As for the title, you'll want to include your primary keyword in the main title of your site (on the home page), and then other keywords you are targeting in the titles of the posts. This will help you to rank higher because, once again, Google's bots will be able to see that your site is relevant for those keywords, and will use this information to properly index your site.

To illustrate this point, I've included an image of the banner and navigation menu of my juicing site. You'll note that the URL is "bestjuicingpractice.com", which includes my full long tail keyword.

My navigation menu is also keyword-rich. The home page includes my primary targeted keyword, while all of the other pages include their respective keywords. For instance, the second page includes the keyword "basics of juicing", wherein I feature a number of posts geared toward the most fundamental aspect of juicing (all of which include their own carefully chosen keyword).

Page Title. You'll also have to carefully craft your page titles. The mistake that most niche site builders make is that they only include a keyword-rich title on their main home page. However, that isn't fully taking advantage of the ranking opportunity that you're being given. Instead, include a page title for every single page of your site, as well as meta tags and descriptions. Really take the time to think about the keywords that you want to focus on, as this is going to determine how quickly you rank. Remember, if you choose a keyword that's too competitive, you are going to find it challenging to beat out more established niche sites.

Targeted Keywords in Content. Last, but certainly not least, you'll want to include the right amount of keywords in the body of your text. Your content should have the proper keyword density (2.5 keyword mentions for every 100 words), and should flow naturally. Don't try to cram them in where they really don't fit. In fact, a trick that I always use when creating content is to read it out loud when I'm done. This allows me to get a better sense of whether or not the piece sounds natural, or if I need to work on keyword integration a bit more before I post the content.

Ultimately, you want to optimize each and every post that you upload to your site. You want to treat every single article or blog post as an opportunity to generate traffic and raise your rank in the major search engines. Each one should have an image, as I mentioned before, with its own description and meta tag. Every piece of content should be treated as though it is your golden opportunity to finally reach number one on that search results page.

Take time to go over all of your posts individually and add in each of these elements that I've discussed if you already have a site. If your site is brand new, then don't hesitate to labor over every page of content to make it just right. Remember, the work you put into it is going to greatly determine what you get out of it.

Chapter 6. Off-Page SEO

Let me begin by saying that, by far, this is the biggest topic that I've mentioned in this book thus far. This is mainly due to the fact that off-page SEO is how we link our niche site to the vast world wide web. It's what takes our site from an isolated blip on the radar, to a significant online presence that is tapped into an extensive network of other sites. So, in this stage of the game, we are actually going to use off-page SEO techniques to link our site to the web.

I often think of this as a spider's web, with thousands of thin silk lines. Each of these lines, which have been carefully spun, are what connects us to sites that have the potential to bring in a new, fresh audience. It's our goal to build and strengthen those thin lines (our connection to other sites), so that they all direct back to the center (our niche site). Ultimately, the more lines you can build, the stronger your niche sites will become.

The Basics of Off Page SEO. There are a number of techniques involved in off-page SEO. Link building is the strategy that is often commonly associated with this type of SEO. However, social media and social bookmarking are also key in any successful off-page SEO campaign. In a nutshell, Off page SEO can be used to improve your ranking and visibility by generating traffic from outside sources. For example, if you include your link in your signature when posting on a forum, this would be considered as a form of off page SEO.

The reason why this type of SEO is so important is primarily due to the fact that it provides search engines with a good indication of just how your website is perceived by web users. Sites that have links from other sites, are bookmarked and shared within niche communities, and have numerous mentions on various social media platforms, such as Facebook, are seen as sites that are relevant within that niche.

I'll be discussing social media and social bookmarking in the next chapter. So, I'm going to focus on link building in this particular section of the book, and how you can create inbound and out bound links for your niche site. Link building is, as the name suggests, building a network of links that redirect to your site, as well as links that direct visitors to other sits outside of your main URL. Inbound links (which are also known as backlinks) can significantly increase traffic to your site and are a great way to boost your online presence.

Types of Link Building. Ideally, you should aim on building a vast network of external links that redirect to your site. By doing this, you can edge out your competition, given that visitors won't even have to use a search engine to find you. For example, if a visitor checks out one of my blogs and decides to place a link to a post I've recently uploaded on their site, Google sees this as an indication that my site has valuable information and will rank it higher. Here are a few of the types of links that you'll want to utilize in order to create that extensive web or traffic generating links:

Forum Signatures. A great way to redirect people to your site is to post on forums and include a link to your site in your signature. This can allow you to build a link, without seeming too "pushy" or "gimmicky" about it. Be sure to carefully craft your forum post, however, as a poorly written one can deter people from actually clicking on your link.

Comment Links on Other Related Sites. This is sort of like a forum signature link, but involves commenting on another site's blog post or article and including a link to relevant information on your site within your response.

Article Directories. I've mentioned article directories before, but wanted to touch on the linking aspect of them here. Submitting an article that contains a link to your site is a great way to create a backlink. Make sure that it's relevant to the topic you're writing about though, as some article directory sites will verify that it's not just a "spam" link.

Link Exchange Agreements. You can get in touch with another web master and see if they are willing to post a link to your site, in exchange for an outgoing link to their site. This can allow you to build an extensive network of links, and can be a valuable strategy if the other site sees quite a bit of traffic.

I highly recommend that you don't just one of the above strategies, but all of them in some way, shape or form. This will enable you to create backlinks that not only draw in new visitors, but send a clear message to the search engines that your site is a relevant and valuable source of information within your niche (and that they need to boost your ranking).

Submitting Your Sites to Directories. You'll also want to submit your site to a number or different directories. This will speed up the indexing process, and allow the major search engines to find you more quickly. The first one you'll want to add your site to is Google, given that they are the most popular search engine. Their sign up process is simple and straightforward...

Google's Submission site is http://www.google.com/submityourcontent/website-owner/ (which is featured in the screen shot below). You'll just need to click on the "Add Your URL" option, and then you'll be able to add your site to their search engine index.

Google will also ask you for a description of your site. Be sure to include keywords in this description, as it's a great opportunity to increase ranking.

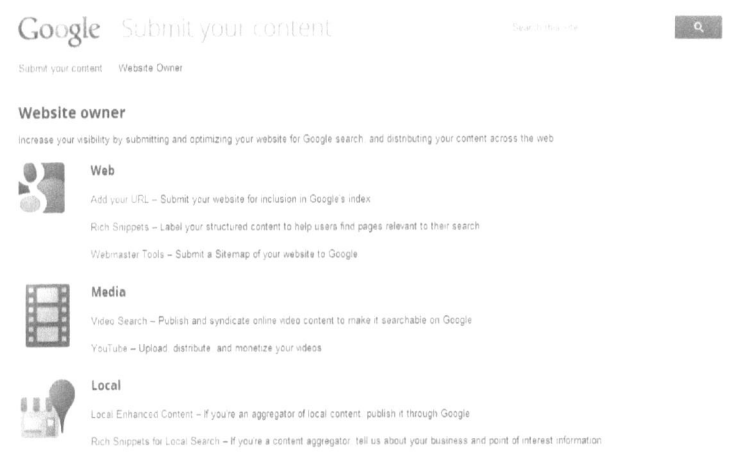

Next you'll want to submit your site to Bing (http://www.bing.com/toolbox/submit-site-url).

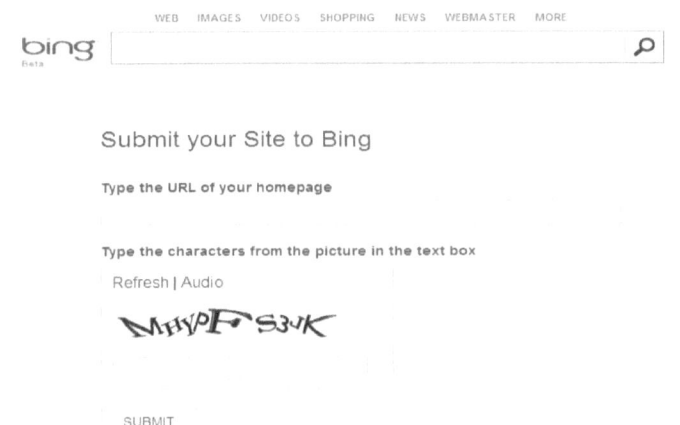

You can also opt to add your site via Bing's web master tool, as well, which allows you to provide more detail about your site. If you want to just submit the URL though, then use the method I mentioned above.

In addition to these major search engines, I strongly recommend that you submit to some other relevant directories as well. Here are just a couple of the ones that you may want to add your niche site to in order to be indexed:

- Stumble Upon-

http://www.stumbleupon.com/submit/visitor (create an account first)

- DMOZ (Open Directory Project)-

http://www.dmoz.org/add.html

You can also submit your sitemap (not your URL) to Ask.com. To do that you don't need to visit their site, instead, just copy and paste this into your browser (with your domain name inserted accordingly):

http://submissions.ask.com/ping?sitemap=http://<your domain name>/sitemapxml.aspx

Helpful Back linking Tip... Here's a quick back linking strategy that I use on a regular basis for all of my niche websites: Submit a 3 line description about your site using the keyword in the description to the following sites:

1. Bing (http://www.bing.com/blogs/f/)

2. Disqus (Disqus.com)

3. Springer Link (http://link.springer.com/)

4. WordPress (profiles.wordpress.org)

5. Open StreetMap Forum (forum.openstreetmap.org)

6. addons.mozilla.org

7. my.opera.com

8. vimeo.com (if you have any video on your site)

9. netwrok.nature.com

10. groups.drupal.org

11. moodle.org

Please keep in mind that there are hundreds more sites like these. The links I've provided are just a handful of examples. However, these few should be enough to get your site the initial boost it needs. Just remember, you need to come back every so often and do more and newer site back linking, as it should be an ongoing process. Once you build enough of these sites and start making some money, then you can think about hiring a virtual assistant to do this work for you.

Chapter 7. Social Media as SEO

When most web site designers and marketers think of SEO, social media doesn't normally spring to mind. Sure, it's often used as way to keep in touch with friends and business contacts, but these sites can also help you to drive traffic to your site and significantly improve your ranking in the major search engines. So, in this section, I am going to share with you how you can effectively use social media sites, such as Twitter and Facebook, to take your SEO strategy to the next level.

Some of the top social media sites that you should be using are: Facebook, Twitter, Google +, and Pinterest. I highly recommend that you create pages on each of these sites for your niche site. There are a number of advantages to doing this. Not only are you able to fully engage your target audience and draw them to your site, but you also make your site more relevant within your niche (leading to improved rankings).

Social media sites allow you to engage potential site visitors, so that they are more likely to share your site with others and read your content themselves. If you have high quality content, then they are more likely to tweet about it, post it on their Facebook page, or add it to their Google + page. If they mention you on their social media profiles or pages, then this boosts your credibility, and goes a long way in terms of ranking.

By adding links to your social media pages you can increase your backlink count and create an even more expansive network of links to your site, which (as I talked about in the last chapter) can dramatically help your ranking in the major search engines. In turn, it's crucial that you place a link to your social media pages on your website, as well, so that loyal visitors can then join you on there and share your site with all of their friends and contacts. Also, encourage visitors to like your page, if applicable.

To help you get started, here are some links to the top social media sites that I recommend you sign up with for your niche site (they are all absolutely free):

Facebook (https://www.facebook.com/)

Twitter (https://twitter.com/)

Pinterest (https://www.pinterest.com/)

Google + (https://plus.google.com/)

Linkedin (http://www.linkedin.com/)

What is Social Bookmarking and Why is it So Important for SEO?

Social bookmarking allows people to search for and manage what are referred to as "bookmarks", which are web pages that they find useful. They then save these links to they would like to view later or share with others via social bookmarking sites, like Delicious (https://delicious.com/) and Digg (digg.com).Users of these sites can view the bookmarks of others, and then (hopefully) be tempted to visit that site.

A vast majority of these sites feature "tags", which are keywords that users can associate with the sites that they like. As such, other users are able to view bookmarks that are linked to a specific keyword tag, and then even see information about the people who have chosen to bookmark the site. Now that we've gone over the basics of what social bookmarking is though, let's talk about exactly why you'll want to integrate it into your SEO strategy for your niche site.

You see, social bookmarking can give you the opportunity to drive high quality traffic to your site. Generally, the visitors that you get from these sites are there because they were looking for a particular topic, and your niche web page showed up as something that might be of interest to them. This can lead to increased monetization revenue. Search engines also pay attention to what's being bookmarked, and actually display bookmarked sites in the search results list. Therefore, bookmarking can also directly improve your rank.

Overall, social bookmarking enables you to draw targeted traffic to your site, rather than just trying to attract anyone and everyone who may be interested in viewing your content. This means that your site will become more relevant within your chosen niche, and that the search engines will pay heed to the fact that your site is a credible source of information about your specific topic, which boost rankings.

Helpful tip: I highly recommend that you go to Socialmarker.com and bookmark your site there. It's a service that gives you the ability to submit your niche site and/or web page to social bookmarking and social news sites, such as Delicious, Reddit, Stumbleupon, and Digg all at once (which will save you a great deal of time).

Chapter 8. How to Promote and Market your site

After you've posted SEO articles and blogs on your niche site and have carried out all of the other items that I've mentioned in this book, it's time to start promoting and marketing. Now, I have to say that this is where a lot of niche internet marketers go wrong. They launch a site and think that they can then just sit back and watch the revenue roll in without any sort of promotion. That couldn't be further from the truth. In fact, I am here to definitively tell you that, if you want your sites to become successful, you are going to have to work toward raising your rank on a continuous basis.

That's not to say that you'll have to devote hours every day to each of your sites, because all of the marketing tips and ideas that I've included in this chapter can be done relatively quickly (and involve very little effort, to be honest). The most difficult part is just staying consistent, and keeping your determination to see your site eventually reach that coveted number one spot (or get very close to it).

Here are some of the niche site promotion insider tips that I have for you. Once you build your site and make it go live, there are few ways you can make the site visible in the eyes of search engines sooner rather than later. These steps help you rank your site faster and can allow you to establish a strong online presence:

1. Put out Press releases. There are many sites that do press releases and they can help any new site become visible to Google and Bing. If you don't want to write one on your own, then hire a freelance writer to craft a professional press release on your behalf.

2. Create a mini YouTube video about your site. Try to be creative when you do this, you can get this done from

Fiverr.com for about $10. Be sure to include a link to your site in the description of the video and in the annotations.

3. **Add new content to the site periodically.** Google keeps an eye out for how often a site is being updated. If you upload more regularly, you have a higher likelihood of being deemed as "relevant" in your niche (this equals an improved chance of ranking toward the top).

4. **Run Free ads.** There are a number of free web classified sites, like Craigslist.com, backpage.com. They don't charge you a dime to post an ad, and you have the potential to reach an entirely new audience.

5. **Directory submission.** Find at least 8-10 related directories and submit your site (the more the better). However, keep in mind not to submit all in one day or one week. Your goal is not to over saturate the web or make it look unnatural. So, space your submissions and don't

overdo it.

6. If possible, Offer something free in your site. It could be a PLR book you bought on your topic for $15, or a free newsletter than you send once a month. You'll offer this item in exchange for a email address. This way you can also build up an email list of individuals who you market to later on.

7. Sign up for a Slideshare.com account. After you register, put up a slide about your site. You will be surprised by just how fast this can show up in Google search results.

8. Sign up for Squidoo.com account. After you've created an account, don't hesitate to mention your niche site to maximize your exposure.

9. Sign up for WordPress.com. Put up a smaller blog

similar to your site, but do not use the same content. This can catch any traffic that your main site may be missing out on.

10. Sign up for other blog sites. Blog platforms like Weebly.com , HubPages.com, Blogger.com, LiveJournal.com, reddit.com and Digg.com can allow you to reach a much wider target audience in your niche.

Chapter 9. Free SEO Tools I use

In the internet marketing world, you have to keep an constant eye on how your sites are doing from Google to alexa rankings. Also to keep an eye on the overall health and performance of the sites. To do this you need to get familiar with some of the tools of the trade I mentioned below.

Use a browser that allows toolbar and extensions to be installed. For example I use Firefox and I use 4 toolbars where I get a wealth of information about any site I visit including my own. here is a screen shot of my toolbars:

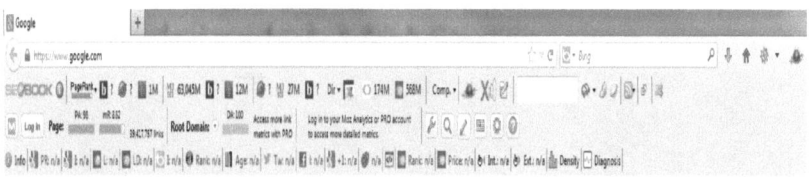

SEO toolbar

MozBar

Seo Quake

WebRank toolbar

Every one of these toolbars in unique in what they offer. Try them and you will see what a difference they can make.

You should also start using Google Web Master Tools, link your sites to it. This way you will have instant knowledge of what keywords your sites are ranking for, where they are ranking and if there are any errors on your site.

These following free sites are what I use to check my own site and to compare my sites with their competitors, these are great tools to 'spy' on your competitors, see what their sites are ranking for and compare that data to your site's data.

1. SEM Rush (http://www.semrush.com)

2. Majestic SEO (http://www.majesticseo.com)

3. Open site Explorer (http://www.opensiteexplorer.org)

SEO Check list for your Niche sites

I'm going to leave you with an easy to follow check list (one that you can even give it to Virtual Assistant to follow if you just don't have the time):

_____Select a Niche that Isn't Overly Competitive or a Micro-Niche Within a Competitive Topic

_____Conduct In-Depth Keyword Research to find Ideal Long Tail Keywords or Phrases

_____Put together a list of top keywords that you will use in future blog posts and articles

_____Design Your Site on WordPress (Using a Theme In-Line with Your Site Goals)

_____Install the WP Plugins that I mentioned earlier in the book (All in one SEO pack, etc)

_____Craft high quality content that includes the proper keyword density

_____Include images on each of your posts (with meta tag descriptions)

_____Create keyword-rich meta tags, descriptions, and heading tags

_____Provide articles to the major article submission sites (for exposure)

_____Implement a link building and social bookmarking strategy

_____Submit your site to search engine directories

_____Create a social media account for your sites and visit Socialmarker.com

_____Put out press releases to promote your sites

_____Upload a short YouTube video to market your niche blog

_____Add new content to your site periodically to improve ranking

****Also, if you're interested, you can go to my site and sign up for my email updates. Since Google changes it's algorithms often, these SEO processes will be updated, and I will email you with any updates on this process regularly (for free)****

Also I am working on a weekly task checklist for my SEO VA, sign up at my site to download this excel file when I am done, this way you can just forward it to your VA to follow and have them send you a report every week.

Last but not the least, if you think I have added some value to your SEO knowledge, please post a review for me. You can always email me and tell me what I can add in my future editions to add more value to this book.